# The Entertainment Ministry

PRESENTS

# The Beverly HILLBILLIES BIBLE STUDY

volume 1

*student guide*

WRITER: *Stephen Skelton*

CREATIVE: *Jim Howell, Judy Northcutt Gaertner*

## *The Beverly Hillbillies* BIBLE STUDY, *volume 1*
## PUBLISHED BY *The Entertainment Ministry, LLC*

Printed in the United States of America

ISBN 0-9707798-0-1

To order or receive more information: *1-800-999-0101 x 136*
*www.entertainmentministry.com*

# FOREWORD

Often, Jesus made his point with a parable—an earthly story with a heavenly meaning. By using real-life situations, his lessons became more relevant and memorable to his listeners. Interestingly, Jesus used parables to allow sincere seekers to understand the message, while others only heard stories without meaning.

For generations afterward, church speakers continued to illustrate Biblical principles using personal anecdotes. With the advent of the press, books and newspapers provided new sources for stories. In the emerging media age, film and radio proved two more. More recently, television rose in prominence.

For the first time, class leaders began to use electronic visual aids, such as scenes from popular movies or television shows. Such high-profile material insured interest. Well-known characters increased the significance. And universal familiarity created community among the audience.

Building from this perspective, it seemed a message could receive a more comprehensive review by screening an entire television episode. Thus, a Bible class based on a specific program seemed a natural progression to the writers of *The Andy Griffith Show Bible Study Series*. A warm reception for that Bible class encouraged work on the next media/ministry study.

At its heart, *The Beverly Hillbillies Bible Study* highlights a simple family, in a world obsessed with money, who try to stay true to their values. Throughout, the show humorously points up the ridiculous adjustments that these plain folk must make to life in the fast lane. Yet, despite their ritzy zip code, the Hillbillies forever hold steadfast to their humble roots and virtues.

From participants of these studies, the comment heard most often is "Using these episodes as parables is not only entertaining, but also broadly appealing, relevant and enriching!" As Christians, there are three main influences in our lives: Faith, Family and Friends. Our hope is that God will use this Bible study to impact you and those with whom you share it.

Blessings,

Stephen Skelton
The Entertainment Ministry

## ABOUT THE AUTHOR

**Stephen Skelton**, co-creator of *The Andy Griffith Show Bible Study Series*, serves as host for *The Beverly Hillbillies Bible Study*. Previously, he has served as a writer-producer with Dick Clark Productions and later as head writer for the television program *America's Dumbest Criminals*. As a Christian in the entertainment industry, Stephen seeks to provide entertainment for edification. To fulfill this mission, The Entertainment Ministry joins ministry and media to impact Christians in their everyday lives. Stephen lives in Nashville, Tennessee with his wife Ashlee and their daughter.

## ABOUT THE ENTERTAINMENT MINISTRY

In the book of Matthew, Jesus says his followers are the salt of the earth and the light of the world. Of course, we know salt seasons and light illuminates. As Christians, we are salt and light when we influence our culture, and one of the most powerful persuaders in our culture is entertainment. Accordingly, The Entertainment Ministry promotes a grassroots approach to engaging entertainment through a Christian worldview. It is our prayer that this practice will bless you, and through you, the world.

# TABLE OF CONTENTS

## THE STORY

This episode, *"The Clampetts Strike Oil,"* introduces
the story of a man named Jed, a poor mountaineer,
who barely kept his family fed.  Until one day,
he was shooting at some food… and the rest is history.
Hillbilly that is!  After a hard life in the mountains,
Jed heads for the good life in Beverly Hills when
he sells his oil-filled swamp for $25 million and
moves his family to the kinder climate of California.

## THE MORAL OF THE STORY

*This lesson, "Count Your Many Blessings,"
highlights the Bible principle of Blessings.
The notes examine the central relationship
between faith and blessings.  This study also
addresses how blessings are best utilized and
what effect blessings should have on us.
In summary form, this lesson underlines
the fundamental reasons why God blesses us.*

# The *Beverly* HILLBILLIES BIBLE STUDY

### volume 1 • lesson 1

EPISODE TITLE: "The Clampetts Strike Oil"

LESSON TITLE: "Count Your Many Blessings"

BIBLICAL THEME: Blessings

## LESSON ONE
# "Count Your Many Blessings"

<u>Unit Overview</u>

## Parable

*Listen to the Story…*

> JEREMIAH 29:11
>
> *"For I know the plans I have for you," declares the LORD, "plans to prosper you and not to harm you, plans to give you hope and a future." (NIV)*

## Reflection

*First Thing You Know…*

> PROVERBS 3:9-10
>
> *Honor the LORD with your wealth, with the firstfruits of all your crops; then your barns will be filled to overflowing, and your vats will brim over with new wine. (NIV)*

## Action

*Load Up Your Truck…*

> 2 CORINTHIANS 9:11
>
> *You will be made rich in every way so that you can be generous on every occasion, and through us your generosity will result in thanksgiving to God. (NIV)*

# Blessings

> JEREMIAH 29:11
>
> *"For I know the plans I have for you," declares the* L<small>ORD</small>,
> *"plans to prosper you and not to harm you, plans to give you*
> *hope and a future." (NIV)*

To most people in the world, being blessed means *"living the good life"*: accomplishing goals and acquiring wealth – with *"accomplishing goals"* being optional. But as measured by God, being blessed first involves faithfulness. When we let God provide our agenda, he works through us to accomplish his purpose. For those committed to his obedience, he has plans for prosperity, hopefulness and a glorious, even eternal, future.

## Parable

### *Listen to the Story…*

Before the other, more worldly folks told them, the Hillbillies didn't know they weren't blessed. The Clampetts were too busy appreciating the little joys of life: family, friends, the oil swamp. Now they have 25 million more blessings to count – talk about good fortune. Briefly, describe the things each character would call blessings in their lives.

**Jed:** _____

**Granny:** _____

**Elly May:** _____

**Jethro:** _____

**Cousin Pearl:** _____

**Mr. Brewster:** _____

**Mr. Drysdale:** _____

**Miss Hathaway:** _____

The premiere of The Beverly Hillbillies captured nearly half of the entire viewing audience in America.

What is the biggest blessing
in your life?  Why?

_____

_____

_____

_____

_____

***To be blessed with anything, we should be thankful in everything
(1 Th 5:16-18).*** *Consider the example of the Hillbillies before
Beverly Hills, when they still lived in the Ozark Mountains.*

Was Jed dissatisfied with life in the mountains?  Should he have been?

_____

_____

_____

***When we acknowledge that God provides everything for us,
we develop a greater appreciation for what He has already
given us (1 Ti 6:17).*** *Thereafter, our gratitude to God will influence
what we do with the next blessing He provides.*

Why did Jed use the money to move?  How did Cousin Pearl
convince him?

_____

_____

_____

_____

Creator Paul Henning
thought up the show
after visiting
Abraham Lincoln's
cabin in Kentucky.

5

***Too often, when a blessing occurs, we give credit to the blessed
instead of the Blesser (Ps 49:16).*** *This misdirected praise can cut two ways:
we put the blessed on a pedestal or the blessed climbs up there all
by himself. Compare the Clampetts' actions to Mr. Drysdale's reaction.*

Did the money change the Clampetts? Why?

_____

_____

_____

_____

How did Mr. Drysdale treat the Clampetts? Why?

_____

_____

_____

_____

_____

_____

ABC turned down
The Beverly Hillbillies
twice without
ever watching
the first episode.

## Reflection

*First Thing You Know...*

PROVERBS 3:9-10
**Honor the LORD with your wealth, with the firstfruits of all your crops; then your barns will be filled to overflowing, and your vats will brim over with new wine.** *(NIV)*

Buddy Ebsen
(Jed Clampett)
had studied the life
of Abraham Lincoln,
written a play
about the President
and sought to play
Lincoln on film.

**With all blessings, wealth, crops or otherwise, we should think of God first and ourselves second. This is the fundamental message of the firstfruits offering (Dt 26:9-11).** When we give first as God would have us, we overcome selfishness, better manage his resources and prepare ourselves to receive more blessings. After all, God doesn't want just the leftovers, possum innards or otherwise.

Like Jed with his family, do you help others before self? Give an example.

_____

_____

_____

_____

Like Cousin Pearl and her truck, have you given away a possession?
Give an example.

_____

_____

_____

_____

*Granny didn't want to go to Cali-for-nie, that promised land of mink and money, even though the warmer weather would be better for her.* **Likewise, we sometimes miss out on a "good thing" from God because it's a "different thing" from God. When in doubt, pray for discernment (Pr 3:5-6).**

Like Granny, have you ever missed or resisted a potential blessing? Give an example.

_____

_____

_____

_____

*Humorously, the Clampetts mistook their mansion for a prison. On a serious note,* **even a blessing can become a burden if handled the wrong way (Dt 11:26-28).** *With blessings come responsibilities.*

Like the Clampetts, have you had a situation seem to go from blessing to curse? Give an example.

_____

_____

_____

_____

Irene Ryan (Granny) once stated, "One of the great joys as Granny is the way children take to me."

The Beverly Hillbillies' mansion was actually located in Bel Air.

8

# Action
## *Load Up Your Truck...*

**2 CORINTHIANS 9:11**
*You will be made rich in every way so that you can be generous on every occasion, and through us your generosity will result in thanksgiving to God.* (NIV)

*We will be blessed so that we can bless others. Those we help will praise God and pray for us. Thus, as we bless others, we will be blessed again. **Giving in this way, we will build up eternal treasures for ourselves, so that our generosity here will be rewarded in heaven (1 Ti 6:18-19).** In the end, any blessing is a blessing only if we use it in the way God intended.*

When is wealth a blessing?

_____

_____

_____

_____

_____

How will you handle the next blessing you receive?

_____

_____

_____

_____

_____

_____

In what way should a blessing change you?

_____

_____

_____

_____

_____

_____

What specific blessing do you want?
Have you prayed for it?

_____

_____

_____

_____

Bea Benaderet
(Cousin Pearl)
was originally chosen
to play Granny...

...Later, the role
of Pearl Bodine
was written
especially for her.

## THE STORY

This episode, *"Getting Settled,"* shows what happens
when the Clampetts arrive at their mansion and encounter
a cement cattle pond, a stove with no stovepipe, and
one lone "chicken"—with pink feathers and stretch legs too!
On top of all that, Miss Hathaway from the bank mistakes
the whole family for a staff of incompetent, countrified servants.
Lucky for the Clampetts, there's no place like home!

## THE MORAL OF THE STORY

*This lesson, "$25 Million & Change," examines
the Biblical principal of Change. The notes focus on
how our trust in God's timing determines our attitude
toward change. The study also spotlights the best ways
in which to deal with trials that arise from change.
The goal of this lesson is to provide perspective on
the place of change in our daily lives.*

# The *Beverly* HILLBILLIES BIBLE STUDY

## volume 1 • lesson 2

EPISODE TITLE: **"Getting Settled"**

LESSON TITLE: **"$25 Million & Change"**

BIBLICAL THEME: **Change**

LESSON TWO

# "$25 Million & Change"

## Unit Overview

## Parable

*Listen to the Story...*

> **ECCLESIASTES 3:1, 2b**
>
> *There is a time for everything, and a season for every activity under heaven: ... a time to plant and a time to uproot.* (NIV)

## Reflection

*First Thing You Know...*

> **PSALM 31:15**
>
> *My times are in your hands; deliver me from my enemies and from those who pursue me.* (NIV)

## Action

*Load Up Your Truck...*

> **MALACHI 3:6a**
>
> *I the LORD do not change.* (NIV)

# Change

ECCLESIASTES 3:1, 2b

*There is a time for everything, and a season for every activity under heaven: ... a time to plant and a time to uproot.* (NIV)

Most of us can't stand change. Or we can't wait for things to be different. Either way, peace comes when we acknowledge and accept God's perfect timing. The alternative, to ignore or reject God's schedule, only leads to despair, or worse, danger. Whether resistant to change or impatient for it to come, we should remember that change itself is only temporary, while God is always constant.

## Parable

### Listen to the Story...

For Hill-folk in the modern world, change is uniquely difficult, if not good for a few laughs. Nevertheless, the Clampetts meant business when they set out to tackle their new surroundings. Comically, what some of them lacked in patience, they made up for in perseverance. Briefly, describe the biggest change each character faced.

**Jed:** _____

**Granny:** _____

**Elly May:** _____

**Jethro:** _____

**Mr. Drysdale:** _____

**Miss Hathaway:** _____

One short month after it premiered, The Beverly Hillbillies was the Number One show on TV.

What changes have you experienced?
How did you handle them?

_____

_____

_____

_____

_____

*Often, change brings challenge.* **When we accept change with faith,**
**we handle trials with patience and a fresh approach** *(2 Th 1:4).*
*When we deny change, we become impatient and revert to old patterns of*
*behavior. Recall how Granny and Jed each handled change.*

How did Granny handle her new kitchen?

_____

_____

_____

_____

_____

Paul Henning,
creator of
The Beverly Hillbillies,
also created
Petticoat Junction
and co-created
Green Acres.

How did Jed react to Elly May's growing up?

_____

_____

_____

_____

_____

*Even when we accept change, it still may not go easy on us—which is still okay.* **God uses obstacles in life to develop our perseverance, which strengthens our character through faith, which fills us with hope for the future with Him** *(Ro 5:3-4).*

What was the outcome of Jethro versus the "pink chicken"? Why?

_____

_____

_____

_____

*Of course, change can be made for the better too. For example,* **where old actions were wrong, new actions could be righteous** *(Jer 7:5-7). Consider how Miss Hathaway changed course with the Clampetts.*

In the end, how did Miss Hathaway deal with the Clampetts? Why?

_____

_____

_____

At first, CBS wanted to change the name of the show to Head for the Hills.

## Reflection

*First Thing You Know...*

> PSALM 31:15
> *My times are in your hands;*
> *deliver me from my enemies*
> *and from those who pursue me.*
> *(NIV)*

*Tellingly, the Bible indicates that **life is both full of change and full of trouble (Job 14:1-2).** Thankfully, God controls our circumstances and he cares deeply for us. **Faith in his greater scheme should keep us from operating on our own timetable (1 Pe 5:6).** To put the situation in perspective, consider that after a time in this ever-changing world, God has offered an eternal life in paradise.*

Like Granny, do you become impatient in new circumstances?
Give an example.

_____

_____

_____

_____

_____

_____

_____

_____

_____

*Elly May received advice from her father. Mr. Drysdale provided assistance to his new neighbors. Just as God guides us in change, often our family and friends can give support.* **Fittingly, this relationship is an extension of our fellowship with the Lord (Ro 1:12).**

Like Elly May, has someone helped you through personal change? Give an example.

_____

_____

_____

_____

Like Mr. Drysdale, have you helped someone else with a change? Give an example.

_____

_____

_____

_____

_____

_____

_____

_____

_____

Granny's given name is Daisy Moses.

The father of Donna Douglas (Elly May Clampett) actually worked for an oil company.

18

*Miss Hathaway made Elly May a maid by mistake (say that three times fast). In a similar fashion, change is not always necessary or even right. As always,* **seek the will of the Lord (Ro 12:2).** *The best change is a blessed change.*

Like Elly May, have you reversed a change that wasn't right?
Give an example.

_____

_____

_____

_____

_____

_____

## Action
### *Load Up Your Truck...*

MALACHI 3:6a
**I the L ORD do not change.** *(NIV)*

*Unlike daily life, the Lord will never change. In a quicksilver world, we can trust our unchanging Christ,* **who is the same yesterday, today and forever (Heb 13:8).** *Change may be inevitable, but God's final victory is certain and everlasting. Though it is difficult to wait when we want change or change when we do not want to,* **God promises that if we submit to him, he will exalt us (Ps 37:34).**

How will you handle the next change in your life?

_____

_____

_____

How will you deal with trials arising from change?

_____

_____

_____

How will you keep change
in perspective?

_____

_____

_____

_____

_____

_____

What do you want to change in your life?  Have you prayed for it?

_____

_____

_____

_____

_____

Nancy Kulp
(Jane Hathaway)
originally wanted
to be a newscaster...

...After Hillbillies, she
ran for Congress
on the Democratic
ticket in
Pennsylvania,
unsuccessfully.

## THE STORY

This episode, *"The Clampetts Meet Mrs. Drysdale,"*
involves a misunderstanding after Mr. Drysdale asks
the Hillbillies to hide their still from his wife, and
the Clampetts assume Mrs. Drysdale must be a drinking woman.
Meanwhile, Mr. Drysdale knows she's not a sot—just a snob
—and works to keep his wife and the new neighbors far apart.
It's "keeping up with the Joneses" Hillbilly style!

## THE MORAL OF THE STORY

*This lesson, "The Truth, The Whole Truth &
Nothing But a Pack of Lies," highlights the
Bible principle of Truth. The notes look at
the benefits of truth versus the tragic cost of lies.
This study also examines the hows and whys of honesty.
The core message of this lesson is that we must
constantly seek—and then safeguard—the truth.*

# The Beverly HILLBILLIES BIBLE STUDY

### volume 1 • lesson 3

EPISODE TITLE: **"The Clampetts Meet Mrs. Drysdale"**

LESSON TITLE: **"The Truth, The Whole Truth & Nothing But a Pack of Lies"**

BIBLICAL THEME: **Truth**

## LESSON THREE
# "The Truth, The Whole Truth & Nothing But a Pack of Lies"

<u>Unit Overview</u>

## Parable

*Listen to the Story...*

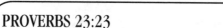

> PROVERBS 23:23
>
> *Buy the truth and do not sell it; get wisdom, discipline and understanding.* (NIV)

## Reflection

*First Thing You Know...*

> PSALM 119:66
>
> *Teach me knowledge and good judgment, for I believe in your commands.* (NIV)

## Action

*Load Up Your Truck...*

> EPHESIANS 4:25
>
> *Therefore each of you must put off falsehood and speak truthfully to his neighbor, for we are all members of one body.* (NIV)

# Truth

> **PROVERBS 23:23**
>
> ***Buy the truth and do not sell it; get wisdom, discipline and understanding.*** *(NIV)*

Ironically, if we're honest, most of us have had trouble with the truth. Whether we've exaggerated it or downplayed it or told half of it or less. Frankly it seems, to tell you the truth—is not always so easy.  But if the truth hurts, lies kill.  Lying destroys trust in marriages, friendships and all other relationships.  Truth, on the other hand, fits with wisdom, discipline and understanding.  Ultimately, God embodies perfect truth, and his Word is completely trustworthy.

## Parable

### *Listen to the Story…*

In this episode, truth takes a holiday —or at least it could sure use a vacation now.  The Hillbillies misunderstood it. Mrs. Drysdale ignored it.  Mr. Drysdale hid it.  And Miss Hathaway finally blurted it out.  Although the Hillbillies still misunderstood it. Briefly, describe the trouble each character had with the truth.

*The Beverly Hillbillies collected a following of 50 million viewers…*

*…And ultimately reached an audience of 65 million.*

**Jed:** _____

**Jethro:** _____

**Granny:** _____

**Mrs. Drysdale:** _____

**Mr. Drysdale:** _____

**Miss Hathaway:** _____

Have you ever had trouble with the truth? What happened?

_____

_____

_____

_____

_____

Buddy Ebsen
(Jed Clampett)
was cast in the
Wizard of Oz, first as
the Scarecrow, and
then the Tin Man,
before falling
ill due to the
silver make-up.

*Sometimes we talk without knowing the whole truth.* **When we jump to assumptions, we lack judgment and deride others (Pr 11:12).** *Think about why Jed said what he said about Mrs. Drysdale.*

What did Jed hear about Mrs. Drysdale? What did he repeat?

_____

_____

_____

*Falsehoods are like avalanches — they bury their witnesses.* **What one person supposes, another person supports — and condemns himself as a false witness (Pr 12:17).** *Consider how Jethro seemed to make the rumor about Mrs. Drysdale more real.*

How did Jethro reply to Jed's claim? Was Jethro right?

_____

_____

_____

25

*While telling lies is obviously wrong, listening to lies is equally as bad. **Liars and their listeners will share the same doomed fate** (Pr 21:28). We must strive to not only speak but actively seek the truth.*

How did Granny respond to Jed and Jethro? What actions did she take next?

_____

_____

_____

_____

_____

_____

How did Mrs. Drysdale view the Clampetts? Initially, what did she base her belief on?

_____

_____

_____

_____

_____

_____

One episode of The Beverly Hillbillies still holds the record for the highest-rated half-hour program.

# Reflection
*First Thing You Know...*

PSALM 119:66

> ***Teach me knowledge and good judgment, for I believe in your commands.*** *(NIV)*

***To favor truth over falsehood, don't tell a lie against anyone*** *(Ex 20:16).* *This is not only the ninth commandment, but the first of three basic steps to defeat falsehoods. The second is **don't spread lies** (Ex 23:1). And the third is, definitively, **don't have anything at all to do with a lie** (Ex 23:7). Indeed, on the day of judgment, **we will have to account for every careless word we have spoken** (Mt 12:36).*

Like the Clampetts, have you acted on a falsehood you accepted as fact? Give an example.

_____

_____

_____

*Jed said it. Jethro confirmed it. And Granny took it for truth. Yet Mrs. Drysdale made up her mind about them even faster. **Lest we also rush to (mis)judgment, our search for the truth should be guided by the wisdom and knowledge we receive through Christ** (Col 2:2-4).*

Like Mrs. Drysdale, have you relied on opinion more than truth? Give an example.

_____

_____

*The Clampetts failed to see the truth. And Mrs. Drysdale saw the truth, but failed to acknowledge it. However, Mr. Drysdale saw the truth, acknowledged it and then had Miss Hathaway try to cover it up! As Christians, **we are instructed to guard the truth** (Ac 20:30-31).*

Like Mr. Drysdale, have you "protected" others from the truth for your benefit?  Give an example.

_____

_____

_____

_____

As a boy, Raymond Bailey (Mr. Drysdale) wanted to be a banker.

Like Miss Hathaway, have you let a lie grow only to make an embarrassing admission?  Give an example.

_____

_____

_____

_____

_____

_____

_____

_____

*Please do not copy.*

28

## Action
### Load Up Your Truck...

EPHESIANS 4:25

*Therefore each of you must put off falsehood and speak truthfully to his neighbor, for we are all members of one body.* (NIV)

*Without a doubt, God holds truthfulness in high regard.* **Twice, with Sodom and Jerusalem respectively, God offers to forgive an entire city for the sake of ten honest people or even one** *(Ge 18:32, Jer 5:1).* *Moreover, throughout the New Testament, the Bible uses the word "truth" to mean God's son Jesus (Jn 14:6). As God's earthly children, while we are promised rewards,* **we are assigned responsibilities in turn— and chief among them is to tell the truth** *(Zec 8:16-17).*

How should you discern the truth?

_____

_____

_____

_____

_____

What steps should you take to guard the truth?

Granny always said she only nipped the jug for medicinal purposes.

_____

_____

_____

_____

_____

Why will you strive to be an honest person?

_____

_____

_____

_____

_____

Is there something you need to tell the truth about?  Why haven't you?

_____

_____

_____

_____

_____

_____

_____

Harriet MacGibbon (Mrs. Drysdale) said her favorite role was Mary, the mother of Jesus, in The Woman at the Tomb.

## THE STORY

This episode, *"Elly Needs a Maw,"* tracks the effects of multiple motives as Jed looks for a maw for Elly, the Widow Fenwick looks for a fellow real estate investor and Mr. Drysdale looks for a way to land both of them at his bank. Plus, Elly and Jethro fight over a hog—of the two-wheeled vehicle variety! It's the tale of the motorcycle, the matchmaker banker and the mismatched millionaires!

## THE MORAL OF THE STORY

*This lesson, **"What's My Motivation?,"** highlights the Bible principle of Motives. The notes examine some essential standards against which to measure our motives. The lesson also looks at the best reasons to commit all of our actions to the Lord. The point of this study is that we should strive to match our own motives to those of our heavenly Father.*

# The Beverly HILLBILLIES BIBLE STUDY

### volume 1 • lesson 4

EPISODE TITLE: **"Elly Needs a Maw"**

LESSON TITLE: **"What's My Motivation?"**

BIBLICAL THEME: **Motives**

## LESSON FOUR
# "What's My Motivation?"

<u>Unit Overview</u>

## Parable

*Listen to the Story...*

1 CHRONICLES 28:9b

*"... For the LORD searches every heart and understands every motive behind the thoughts."* (NIV)

## Reflection

*First Thing You Know...*

PHILIPPIANS 2:3-4

*Do nothing out of selfish ambition or vain conceit, but in humility consider others better than yourselves. Each of you should look not only to your own interests, but also to the interests of others.* (NIV)

## Action

*Load Up Your Truck...*

PROVERBS 16:3

*Commit to the LORD whatever you do, and your plans will succeed.* (NIV)

# Motives

**1 CHRONICLES 28:9b**

*"... For the LORD searches every heart and understands every motive behind the thoughts." (NIV)*

Before we take action, we should ask *"What's My Motivation?"* Like actors who ask that, being "acters" ourselves, we also act from motive. Even when we "don't think before we act," we act from our motives. As Christians, before we have to ask "What Would Jesus Do," we might ask *"What Would Jesus Want?"* Of course, Jesus always wanted to do the will of the Father—to love God and serve others. If this is our fundamental motive, whatever we ask—or act—for will be given to us.

## Parable

### *Listen to the Story...*

Usually, a look at motives spells crime more than comedy—but then nearly everyone here seems guilty of somthing. Only Jed is selfless, while Mr. Drysdale is selfish and Mrs. Fenwick simply sells. Meanwhile, most of the others operate from similarly self-serving agendas. Briefly, describe how each character is motivated.

**Jed:** _____

**Mr. Drysdale:** _____

**Miss Hathaway:** _____

**Mrs. Fenwick:** _____

**Elly May:** _____

**Jethro:** _____

**Granny:** _____

The Beverly Hillbillies claims eight of the Top 50 highest rated programs...

...No other show in the history of television claims more.

How are you best motivated?  Why?

_____

_____

_____

_____

*Our motives may be a mystery to others, but God understands our hearts. Just remember, **because God sees through you, a clear conscience will see you through** (1 Jn 3:21-22).  Consider the way in which Jed worked toward his goal.*

Why did Jed want to take a wife?
Did he make his real reason clear?

_____

_____

_____

_____

_____

_____

_____

*"Business as usual" can make our motives seem neutral.  **It's easy to repeat seemingly acceptable patterns, but God constantly reviews our purpose** (Pr 16:2).  Recall Mrs. Fenwick's actions, then think about her intent.*

Was Mrs. Fenwick hurting anyone?  What was the purpose of her plan?

_____

_____

_____

_____

*Often, we determine whether our motives are realized or rejected.* **We make that choice by living righteously versus acting wickedly (Pr 11:8).** *Depending upon the direction we choose, our actions can make our dreams or our fears happen.*

Why did Mr. Drysdale fail as a matchmaker banker? How might he have succeeded?

_____

_____

_____

_____

_____

As an aspiring actor, Raymond Bailey (Mr. Drysdale) was once fired for trying to sneak into a mob scene.

What did Elly do to scare off the maw she wanted? How might she soothe the next one?

_____

_____

_____

_____

_____

_____

*First Thing You Know...*

PHILIPPIANS 2:3-4

*Do nothing out of selfish ambition or vain conceit, but in humility consider others better than yourselves. Each of you should look not only to your own interests, but also to the interests of others. (NIV)*

Donna Douglas

(Elly May Clampett)

once said,

"I was a pitcher

on the boys'

softball team

for so long,

I was fourteen

before I found out

there was

a girls' team"

One of our primary motives should be to serve. When we serve out of love for God and others, we emulate Jesus, who gave us an excellent example of humility. **Being humble allows us to adjust our perception of self as we lower the emphasis on our own interests (Ro 12:3).** With this attitude, we will seek to give rather than receive. When we put others first, we can always be honest about our motives and therefore open with our actions.

Like Jed, are you open with both your motives and actions?
Give an example.

_____

_____

_____

_____

Like Miss Hathaway, do you seek opportunities to serve others?
Give an example.

_____

_____

_____

_____

*Jethro wanted to (for lack of a better phrase) hog his hog—motorcycle that is. Perhaps it's fitting then that he never got to ride it this entire episode, as that honor went to Elly and even Granny!* **Rather than maintain selfish motives, we should ask God to give us what we need (Jas 4:3).**

Like Jethro, have you turned selfish over a possession? Give an example.

_____

_____

_____

_____

_____

*Elly May never altered her actions, even when her father asked her to. She may have needed a maw, but more than that, she wanted to run wild. As we navigate between want and need,* **our Father strengthens us from within to enable us to accomplish his work (Php 2:13).**

Like Elly May, are you motivated more by want than need? Give an example.

_____

_____

_____

_____

_____

_____

Irene Ryan (Granny) used her money to establish a scholarship fund for theater students throughout the country.

## Action
### *Load Up Your Truck...*

PROVERBS 16:3
**Commit to the LORD whatever you do, and your plans will succeed.** *(NIV)*

*The first test of any motive is to confirm that it is pleasing to God. After all, the final outcome of any action we take is in his hands. For our actions to accomplish God's will, there must be a balance between our motivation and his control. When we commit a plan to the Lord, we should ask if it will accomplish his purpose and make sure our attitude is acceptable.*
**As we begin to do God's will, our desire to see it fulfilled will grow (Php 4:8-9).**

How will you form your motives?

_____

_____

_____

_____

What will one of your main motivations be?

_____

_____

_____

_____

_____

How will you commit to maintain the right motives?

_____

_____

_____

_____

_____

_____

Do your current motives need to be changed?  Explain.

_____

_____

_____

_____

_____

_____

Under her autograph, Donna Douglas (Elly May Clampett) usually writes Proverbs 3:5-6: "Trust in the LORD with all your heart and lean not on your own understanding; in all your ways acknowledge him, and he will make your paths straight."